POPE FRANCIS
AND THE FAMILY

POPE FRANCIS
and the
FAMILY

VERITAS

Published 2015 by
Veritas Publications
7–8 Lower Abbey Street
Dublin 1
Ireland

publications@veritas.ie
www.veritas.ie

ISBN 978 1 84730 653 1

Copyright © Paola Dal Toso, Libreria Editrice Vaticana
Translation of the Italian *Papa Francesco e la famiglia*.
English translation copyright © 2014, Libreria Editrice Vaticana
(LEV), Vatican City State. All rights reserved.

10 9 8 7 6 5 4 3 2 1

The material in this publication is protected by copyright law. Except as may be permitted by law, no part of the material may be reproduced (including by storage in a retrieval system) or transmitted in any form or by any means, adapted, rented or lent without the written permission of the copyright owners. Applications for permissions should be addressed to the publisher.

A catalogue record for this book is available from the British Library.

Designed by Padraig McCormack, Veritas Publications
Printed by Colorman (Ireland) Limited

Veritas books are printed on paper made from the wood pulp of managed forests. For every tree felled, at least one tree is planted, thereby renewing natural resources.

Contents

Introduction 7

Essential for Coexistence and
Necessary for Human Survival 9

The Principal Setting for Growth 11

The Family Today 13

Marriage 15

Mothers and Fathers 19

Children 23

The Role of Grandparents 27

The Wisdom of the Elderly 33

The Culture of Encounter
vs the Culture of Exclusion 35

Relationships 41

Education 45

Dreaming Big 53

Handing on the Faith 63

St Joseph: Protector of the Family of Nazareth . . . 67

Mother Mary 71

God Is a Merciful Father 75

Spiritual Fatherhood and Motherhood 83

God's Family 87

The Whole World Understood as One Big Family . 93

Endnotes 95

Introduction

A mere six months from the beginning of his Petrine ministry on 13 March 2013, one would not have expected much from Pope Francis on the subject of the family. And yet, there has been no shortage of comments. Careful analysis reveals his interventions, homilies and messages to be full of ideas and reflections, although the Holy Father's contributions for consideration are obviously those of a pastor.

This book seeks to offer everything the Holy Father has expressed on various aspects of the family to date, organised as thematically as can be, given the brevity of his magisterium.

The text refers to everything the pope has written or spoken from the beginning of his pontificate until the Solemnity of the Assumption of the Blessed Virgin Mary, celebrated on 15 August 2013, also taking into consideration the content of the meditations offered during the celebrations of the morning Eucharist in the chapel of Casa Santa Marta as reported by *L'Osservatore*

Romano. The endnotes enable the reader to check citations in their complete original form on the official website of the Holy See for further study: *www.vatican.va*.

The frequency with which the pontiff returns to certain questions may give the impression that some thoughts are being repeated. It is rather a matter of concepts being expressed in terms that are sometimes very similar but never identical, even if they appear so to the reader. This shows how certain crucial questions are particularly in Pope Francis' thoughts, an impression that is reinforced by the colloquial tone he often employs, especially when he is speaking to large audiences.

Essential for Coexistence and Necessary for Human Survival

In the magisterium that began on 13 March 2013, Pope Francis has repeatedly addressed the theme of the family and not only from the spiritual perspective. He recognises the family as one of the foundations underlying the common good and makes the point clearly:

> There is neither real promotion of the common good nor real human development when there is ignorance of the fundamental pillars that govern a nation, its non-material goods: *life*, which is a gift of God, a value always to be protected and promoted; the *family*, the foundation of coexistence and a remedy against social fragmentation; *integral education*, which cannot be reduced to the mere transmission of information for purposes of generating profit; *health*, which must seek the integral well-being of the person, including the spiritual dimension, essential

for human balance and healthy coexistence; security, in the conviction that violence can be overcome only by changing human hearts.[1]

The Holy Father states even more clearly: 'Not only would I say that the family is important for the evangelisation of the new world. The family is important, and it is necessary for the survival of humanity. Without the family, the cultural survival of the human race would be at risk. The family, whether we like it or not, is the foundation.'[2]

The Principal Setting for Growth
~~~

Pope Francis reaffirms with conviction that the 'family is the principal setting for the growth of each individual, since it is through the family that human beings become open to life and the natural need for relationships with others. Over and over again we see that family bonds are essential for the stability of relationships in society, for the work of education and for integral human development, for they are inspired by love, responsible intergenerational solidarity and mutual trust. These are factors which can make even the most adverse situations more bearable, and bring a spirit of true fraternity to our world, enabling it to feel as a single family, where the greatest attention is paid to those most in need.'[3]

How can such goals be reached? According to the pontiff, 'Every economic and political theory or action must set about providing each inhabitant of the planet with the minimum wherewithal to live in dignity and freedom, with the possibility of supporting a family, educating children, praising God and developing one's own human potential. This is the main thing.'[4]

Support for the family is also needed to face challenges and the tendency to disintegrate: 'It is very important to reaffirm the family, which remains the essential cell of society and the Church.'[5]

The Family Today

The Holy Father sums up the situation that the family faces today in a brief analysis:

> In Italy too, as in many other countries, the historical period in which we are living is characterised by a profound and persistent global crisis. This crisis accentuates economic and social problems and is weighing most heavily upon the weakest social strata. Particularly alarming are phenomena such as the undermining of the family and of social bonds, demographic decline, the prevalence of types of logic that give priority to profit rather than to work, and insufficient attention to the younger generations and their training, also with a view to a serene and secure future.[6]

He attaches particular importance to the promotion of Christian values 'in a world that seems at times to call into question some of the foundations of society, such as respect for the sacredness of human life or the importance of the institution of the family built on marriage'.[7]

Pope Francis is not unaware of the dramatic situations that people can find themselves going through today. He notes one in particular, on the occasion of the celebration of the Word Day of Refugees, and he makes this appeal:

> This year we are asked to consider in particular the situation of refugee families, often forced to flee their homes and homeland suddenly, losing all their possessions and security in order to escape violence, persecution or grave discrimination because of the religion they profess, the ethnic group they belong to or their political ideas.
>
> In addition to the dangers of migration, these families often risk being broken up and, in the countries that receive them, they must come to terms with cultures and societies different from their own. We cannot be insensitive to the families and to all our brothers and sisters who are refugees. We are called to help them, opening ourselves to understanding and hospitality. May people and institutions that help them never be lacking anywhere in the world; their faces reflect the face of Christ![8]

Marriage

The Christian family is founded upon:

> the stable union of man and woman in marriage. This union is born of their love, as a sign and presence of God's own love, and of the acknowledgment and acceptance of the goodness of sexual differentiation, whereby spouses can become one flesh (cf. Gn 2:24) and are enabled to give birth to a new life, a manifestation of the Creator's goodness, wisdom and loving plan. Grounded in this love, a man and a woman can promise each other mutual love in a gesture which engages their entire lives and mirrors many features of faith. Promising love forever is possible when we perceive a plan bigger than our own ideas and undertakings, a plan which sustains us and enables us to surrender our future entirely to the one we love.[9]

Pope Francis explicitly warns against provisional choices:

All of us, even those of us who are older, even we feel the pressure of this culture of the provisional; and this is dangerous because one never makes life choices once and for all. I'll stay married for as long as the love lasts; I'll become a nun but just for a while ... a little time and then we'll see; I'll be a seminarian to become a priest but I don't know how it will all turn out in the end. Jesus won't have this! It's not you that I'm reproaching, I'm reproaching this culture of the provisional which afflicts us all because it doesn't do us any good, because in this day and age it's very hard to make a definitive choice. In my day it was easier because the culture supported definitive choices whether for married life or for consecrated life or priestly life. But these days a definitive choice is not easy. We are victims of this culture of the provisional.[10]

Consequently, 'Today, there are those who say that marriage is out of fashion. Is it out of fashion? In a culture of relativism and the ephemeral, many preach the importance of "enjoying" the moment. They say that it is not worth making a lifelong commitment, making a definitive decision, "forever", because we do not know what tomorrow will bring.'[11]

The pontiff is well aware that 'it is so hard in our time to make final decisions! ... Temporary things seduce us. We are victims of a trend that pushes us to the provisional ... as though we wanted to stay adolescents. There is a *certain attraction to remaining adolescents our whole lives!* Let us not be afraid of life commitments, commitments that take up and concern our entire life! In this way our life will be fruitful! And this is freedom: to have the courage to make these decisions with generosity.'[12]

The pope further addresses the complex problem of adequate pastoral care for marriage. He does not hide the fact that in some cases people get married without preparation. 'Cardinal Quarracino, my predecessor, used to say that as far as he was concerned, half of all marriages are null. But why did he say this? Because people get married lacking maturity, they get married without realising that it is a lifelong commitment, they get married because society tells them they have to get married. And this is where the pastoral care of marriage also comes in.'[13]

Finally, the Holy Father reminds us that when an engaged couple who wish to get married visit the parish office, it can happen that, instead of support or congratulations, they get a price list for the ceremony or they are asked if their documents are all in order. In this way, sometimes 'they find the door closed'. And so, someone who could have 'opened the door giving thanks to God for this new marriage' does not do so, but rather closes the door.[14]

Mothers and Fathers

Pope Francis asks us always to thank our own parents: 'Each and every one of us owes so much to our earthly father, who handed life on to us, who cared for us, and who continues to provide for our daily existence and growth. Do not forget to give thanks to God for your father! Remember him in prayer, even if your relationship happened not to be good.'[15] He returns again to this theme: 'Let us think: how many dads and mums every day put their faith into practice by offering up their own lives in a concrete way for the good of the family!'[16]

Already, in the course of the life of an unborn child, there is such a close relationship with the parents that 'from our mother's womb we learn to recognise her voice and that of our father; it is from the tone of a voice that we perceive love or contempt, affection or coldness'.[17]

In an effective synthesis, the Holy Father outlines in particular the mother's role in raising children:

A mother helps her children grow up and wants them to grow strong; that is why she teaches them not to be lazy – which can also derive from a certain kind of wellbeing – not to sink into a comfortable lifestyle, contenting oneself with possessions. The mother takes care that her children develop better, that they grow strong, capable of accepting responsibilities, of engaging in life, of striving for great ideals ...

A mother then thinks of the health of her children, teaching them also *to face the difficulties of life*. You do not teach, you do not take care of health by avoiding problems, as though life were a motorway with no obstacles. The mother helps her children to see the problems of life realistically and not to get lost in them, but to confront them with courage, not to be weak, and to know how to overcome them, in a healthy balance that a mother 'senses' between the area of security and the area of risk. And a mother can do this! She does not always take the child along the safe road, because in that way the child cannot develop, but neither does she leave the child only on the risky path, because that is dangerous. A mother knows how to balance things. A life without challenges does not exist and a boy or a girl who cannot face or tackle them is a boy or girl with no backbone![18]

Regarding these difficulties the pope reaffirms: 'Also in the civil context it is true that faith assures us: there is no need to lose hope. How many examples of this have our parents and grandparents given us in their time by facing harsh trials with great courage and a spirit of sacrifice!'[19]

Finally, referring to the maternal figure, he reminds us that a mother does not just accompany her children's growth, but 'also helps them to *make definitive decisions with freedom*. This is not easy, but a mother knows how to do it'.[20]

Children

Pope Francis is anxious 'to continue to pay special attention to this most important issue of respect for human life from the moment of conception. In this regard I would also like to remember the collection of signatures being made today in Italian parishes in support of the European project "One of Us". The initiative aims to guarantee embryos legal protection, safeguarding every human being from the very first moment of his or her existence.'[21]

Sometimes 'well-being anesthetises us' because, when all is said and done, 'we are comfortable being comfortable' and that can often affect the decision to have a child.[22] The pope imagines a conversation between a married couple who are refusing to be fertile: 'No, no, no more than one child, no! Because then we can't go on vacation, we can't go here, we can't buy a house; no! It is all fine and good to follow the Lord but only to a certain point.'[23]

In the history of salvation having children is considered a blessing. 'In Abraham's journey towards the future city, the Letter to the Hebrews mentions the blessing which was passed on from fathers to sons (cf. Heb 11:20-21) … Faith also helps us to grasp in all its depth and richness the begetting of children, as a sign of the love of the Creator who entrusts us with the mystery of a new person. So it was that Sarah, by faith, became a mother, for she trusted in God's fidelity to his promise (cf. Heb 11:11).'[24]

The Holy Father quotes a traditional Brazilian saying and comments: 'Here it is common for parents to say, "Our children are the apple of our eyes." What a beautiful expression of Brazilian wisdom this is, applying to young people an image drawn from our eyes, which are the window through which light enters into us, granting us the miracle of sight! What would become of us if we didn't look after our eyes? How could we move forward?'[25]

In the same spirit, the Holy Father turns to the young people:

> Listen! Young people are the window through which the future enters the world. They are the window, and so they present us with great challenges. Our generation will show that it can rise to the promise found in each young person when we know how to give them space. This means that we have to create the material and spiritual conditions for their full

development; to give them a solid basis on which to build their lives; to guarantee their safety and their education to be everything they can be; to pass on to them lasting values that make life worth living; to give them a transcendent horizon for their thirst for authentic happiness and their creativity for the good; to give them the legacy of a world worthy of human life; and to awaken in them their greatest potential as builders of their own destiny, sharing responsibility for the future of everyone. If we can do all this, we anticipate today the future that enters the world through the window of the young.[26]

Regarding younger children, the pontiff clearly states: 'All children must be able to play, study, pray and grow, in their own families, and do so in a harmonious context of love and serenity. It is their right and our duty. Many people instead of letting them play make slaves of them: this is a scourge. A serene childhood allows children to look forward with confidence to life and the future. Woe to those who stifle their joyful impulse of hope!'[27]

The pope turns his thoughts 'to those who have suffered and are suffering from abuse. I would like to assure them that they are present in my prayers, but I would like to strongly declare that we must all commit ourselves with clarity and courage so that every human person, especially children, who are among the most vulnerable, be always defended and protected.'[28]

Finally, the Holy Father wishes to present the child as a model for us all: 'The gentleness that Jesus wants from us ... is simple, like that of a child; and a child is not hypocritical because he or she is not corrupt. When Jesus tells us, let your speech be yes, yes, no, no, with a child's spirit, he is telling us the opposite of what corrupt people say ...'[29] 'Let us ask the Lord today that our way of speaking may be that of the simple, the language of children, the language of God's children and consequently the language of the truth in love.'[30]

The Role of Grandparents

In a Christian upbringing, the mother has always been a mediator in the relationship between her child and God. Pope Francis also reminds us of this fact: 'This is part of the mission of women; of mothers, of women! Witnessing to their children, to their grandchildren, that Jesus is alive, is living, is risen. Mothers and women, carry on witnessing to this! It is the heart that counts for God, how open to him we are, whether we are like trusting children.'[31]

As for grandmothers, he recognises the important task of witnessing and handing on the gift of the faith. He underscores this while explaining to newly ordained priests the mission to which they have been called: 'Remember your mothers, your grandmothers, your catechists, who gave you the word of God, the faith … the gift of faith! They transmitted to you this gift of faith.'[32]

The Holy Father makes reference to his personal experience, recalling what his grandmother explained to him about the sin that Jesus takes on himself: 'When we were small, our grandmother used to say: a shroud has no pocket.'[33]

He vividly recalls other childhood experiences to make even clearer the message he wishes to communicate and anchor in real life: 'I always remember that on the evening of Good Friday she would take us to the candlelight procession, and at the end of this procession "the dead Christ" would arrive and our grandmother would make us – the children – kneel down and she would say to us: "Look, he is dead, but tomorrow he will rise."'[34] 'The entry into faith is like that – faith in Christ dead and risen.'[35]

Pope Francis shares his own life story:

> I had the great blessing of growing up in a family in which faith was lived in a simple, practical way. However it was my paternal grandmother in particular who influenced my journey of faith. She was a woman who explained to us, who talked to us about Jesus, who taught us the Catechism ... I received my first Christian proclamation, from this very woman, from my grandmother! This is really beautiful! The first proclamation at home, in the family! And this makes me think of the love of so many mothers and grandmothers in the transmission of faith. They are the ones who pass on the faith.

This used to happen in the early Church too, for St Paul said to Timothy: 'I am reminded of the faith of your mother and of your grandmother' (cf. 2 Tm 1:5).[36]

In the same way, the pontiff invites everyone, especially mothers and grandmothers, to hand on faith that does not exist in the abstract but is always proclaimed by a person, as St Paul makes clear in the letter where he speaks to Timothy about the faith '"that which you received from your mother and your grandmother you must pass on to others". This is how we received the faith ourselves, in the family; faith in Jesus.' The foundation and power of the faith lie 'in the risen Jesus, in Jesus who has forgiven our sins by his death and has reconciled us with the Father. Handing this on requires us to be brave: the courage to hand on the faith. A courage that is sometimes simple.'[37]

A grandparent's prayers can help a religious choice blossom and grow. Pope Francis is convinced of this when he says: 'Behind and before every vocation to the priesthood or the consecrated life there is always the strong and intense prayer of someone: a grandmother, a grandfather, a mother, a father, a community …'[38]

On the occasion of the feast of Ss Joachim and Anna, the grandparents of Jesus, which the Church celebrates on 26 July, the Holy Father reaffirms: 'Mary grew up in the home of Joachim and Anne; she was surrounded by their love and faith: in their home she learned to listen to the Lord and to follow his will. Saints Joachim and Anne were part of a long chain of people who had transmitted their faith and love for God, expressed in the warmth and love of family life, down to Mary, who received the Son of God in her womb and who gave him to the world, to us. How precious is the family as the privileged place for transmitting the faith!'[39]

The pontiff also highlights another aspect of the presence of grandparents in the family environment: 'How important grandparents are for family life, for passing on the human and religious heritage which is so essential for each and every society! How important it is to have intergenerational exchanges and dialogue, especially within the context of the family. The *Aparecida Document* says, 'Children and the elderly build the future of peoples: children because they lead history forward, the elderly because they transmit the experience and wisdom of their lives' (no. 447). This relationship and this dialogue between generations is a treasure to be preserved and strengthened!'[40]

Grandparents deserve affectionate thanks for the witness of wisdom that they continue to offer. Pope Francis himself offers proof. Asked about his relationship with his predecessor, Pope Emeritus Benedict XVI, Pope Francis said this: 'I have found a good answer for this:

"It's like having your grandfather in the house", a wise grandfather. When families have a grandfather at home, he is venerated, he is loved, he is listened to ... For me it's like having a grandfather at home: my own father. If I have a difficulty, or something I don't understand, I can call him on the phone: "Tell me, can I do this?""[41]

The Wisdom of the Elderly

Equally interesting are Pope Francis' frequent references to the role of the elderly, while observing that, in Argentina, older people are addressed as 'grandmother' and 'grandfather'.[42] He observes them with great tenderness, admiring their wisdom, 'How many people – so many old people – have taken this path! And it is beautiful to see them: they have that beautiful countenance, that serene happiness. They do not say much, but have a patient heart, a heart filled with love. They know what forgiving enemies means, they know what it is to pray for enemies.'[43]

The Holy Father invites us to follow the example of the elderly to be patient and forbearing. 'Going along patiently renews our youthfulness and makes us younger. A patient person is someone who is younger in the long run! Think about the elderly men and women in a nursing home; those who have put up with so much in the course of their lives; look at their eyes: they are youthful eyes, they have a youthful spirit and a renewed youthfulness. This is what the Lord invites us to.' 44

> This profound respect for the elderly, born of esteem and affection, comes from the conviction that: Old age is – as I like to say – the seat of life's wisdom. The old have acquired the wisdom that comes from having journeyed through life, like the old man Simeon, the old prophetess Anna in the Temple. And that wisdom enabled them to recognise Jesus. Let us pass on this wisdom to the young: like good wine that improves with age, let us give life's wisdom to the young. I am reminded of a German poet who said of old age: *Es is ruhig, das Alter, und fromm*: it is a time of tranquillity and prayer.[45]

> Speaking to seminarians and male and female novices, the pope advises with a hint of irony, 'Do not learn from us, from us who are no longer very young; do not learn from us the sport to which we old men so often have recourse: the sport of complaining! Do not learn from us the cult of the "goddess lamentation". She is a goddess that … is always complaining …'[46]

The Culture of Encounter vs the Culture of Exclusion

Encountering others is always a source of mutual enrichment as long as we know how to approach each other and enter into dialogue with an attitude that is open, available and unprejudiced. Pope Francis reaffirms this with conviction:

> The only way for individuals, families and societies to grow, the only way for the life of peoples to progress, is via the culture of encounter, a culture in which all have something good to give and all can receive something good in return. Others always have something to give me, if we know how to approach them in a spirit of openness and without prejudice. This open spirit, without prejudice, I would describe as 'social humility,' which is what favours dialogue. Only in this way can understanding grow between cultures and religions, mutual esteem without needless preconceptions, in a climate that

is respectful of the rights of everyone. Today, either we take the risk of dialogue, we risk the culture of encounter, or we all fall.[47]

The Holy Father insists: 'We must know how to meet each other. We must build, create, construct a culture of encounter. How many differences, how many problems in the family there always are! Problems in the neighbourhood, problems at work, problems everywhere. And differences don't help. The culture of encounter. Going out to meet each other.'[48]

In another interesting reflection on the culture of encounter, the Holy Father proposes a contrast with its opposite, exclusion, by way of a warning: 'Take care of the two ends of the population: the elderly and the young; do not allow yourselves to be excluded and do not allow the elderly to be excluded',[49] because both groups are 'the hope of a nation; the young, because they bring strength, idealism and hope for the future; the elderly because they represent the memory, the wisdom of the people'.[50] Pope Francis reminds us yet again:

> At the other end of life, the elderly, they too are the future of a people. A people has a future if it goes forward with both elements: with the young, who have the strength, and things move forward because

they do the carrying; and with the elderly because they are the ones who give life's wisdom. And I have often thought that we do the elderly an injustice, we set them aside as if they had nothing to offer us; they have wisdom, life's wisdom, history's wisdom, the homeland's wisdom, the family's wisdom. And we need all this! ... We have become somewhat accustomed to this throwaway culture: too often the elderly are discarded! ... We must rid ourselves of this habit of throwing away. No! The culture of inclusion, the culture of encounter, making an effort to bring everyone into society![51]

The pontiff returns to the social exclusion of the aged and the young referring to the fact that:

> our world civilization ... has made money into such a god that we are now faced with a philosophy and a practice which exclude the two ends of life that are most full of promise for peoples. They exclude the elderly, obviously. You could easily think there is a kind of hidden euthanasia, that is, we don't take care of the elderly; but there is also a cultural euthanasia, because we don't allow them to speak, we don't allow them to act ... the elderly must open their mouths, the elderly must open their mouths and teach us! Pass on to us the wisdom of the peoples! ...

I ask the elderly, from my heart: do not cease to be the cultural storehouse of our people, a storehouse that hands on justice, hands on history, hands on values, hands on the memory of the people. And the rest of you, please, do not oppose the elderly: let them speak, listen to them and go forward. But know this, know that at this moment, you young people and you elderly people are condemned to the same destiny: exclusion. Don't allow yourselves to be excluded.[52]

The Holy Father encourages us yet again to feel ourselves 'to be *called to promote the culture of encounter* – In many places, generally speaking, due to the economic humanism that has been imposed in the world, the culture of exclusion, of rejection, is spreading. There is no place for the elderly or for the unwanted child; there is no time for that poor person in the street.'[53] In short, for the culture of exclusion, 'Everything is disposable. A culture that always leaves people out of the equation: it leaves children out, it leaves young people out, it leaves the elderly out, it leaves out all who are of no use, who do not produce, and this must not be! On the contrary, solidarity includes everyone.'[54]

With heartfelt tones, the pontiff repeats an interesting observation: We must never, never allow the throwaway culture to enter our hearts! We must never allow the throwaway culture to enter our hearts, because we are brothers and sisters. No one is disposable! Let us always remember this: only when we are able to share do we become truly rich; everything that is shared is multiplied! Think of the multiplication of the loaves by Jesus! The measure of the greatness of a society is found in the way it treats those most in need, those who have nothing apart from their poverty![55]

Relationships

While visiting the 'Gift of Mary' Shelter for the Homeless operated by the sisters of Mother Teresa of Calcutta, Pope Francis reminds us that the word '"home" is a word with a typically familiar flavour, which recalls warmth, affection and love that can be felt in a family. Hence the "home" represents the most precious human treasures, that of encounter, that of relations among people, different in age, culture and history, but who live together and together help one another to grow. For this reason, "home" is a crucial place in life, where life grows and can be fulfilled, because it is a place in which every person learns to receive love and to give love.'[56]

The Holy Father asks himself:

> But what is the power that unites the family? It is indeed love, and the One who sows love in our hearts is God, God's love, it is precisely God's love that gives meaning to our small daily tasks and helps us face the great trials. This is the true treasure of

> humankind: going forward in life with love, with that love which the Lord has sown in our hearts, with God's love. This is the true treasure … It is a love that gives value and beauty to everything else; a love that gives strength to the family, to work, to study, to friendship, to art, to all human activity. It even gives meaning to negative experiences, because this love allows us to move beyond these experiences, to go beyond them, not to remain prisoners of evil, it moves us beyond, always opening us to hope.[57]

Interpersonal relationships within the family are not always easy, yet they should always be characterised by:

> the law of love, love for God and love for neighbour according to the new commandment that the Lord left to us (cf. Jn 13:34). It is a love, however, that is not sterile sentimentality or something vague, but the acknowledgment of God as the one Lord of life and, at the same time, the acceptance of the other as my true brother, overcoming division, rivalry, misunderstanding, selfishness; these two things go together. Oh how much more of the journey do we have to make in order to actually live the new law – the law of the Holy Spirit who acts in us, the law of charity, of love! … Even within the family itself, there are so many internal wars![58]

Whenever people are more willing to follow nothing, then 'disputes arise within families, between friends, in society'.[59]

Particularly dear to Pope Francis is the theme of caring, nurturing, protecting and of assuming responsibility. He points out that:

> the vocation of being a 'protector', however, is not just something for Christians alone; it also has a prior dimension which is simply human, involving everyone ... It means protecting people, showing loving concern for each and every person, especially children, the elderly, those in need, who are often the last we think about. It means caring for one another in our families: husbands and wives first protect one another, and then, as parents, they care for their children, and children themselves, in time, protect their parents.[60]

In other words, the pontiff underscores that it is important, 'To embrace, to embrace – we all have to learn to embrace the one in need, as St Francis did. There are so many situations ... that require attention, care and love ... Often, instead, it is selfishness that prevails in our society.'[61]

The relationships that are part of everyone's life, beginning with family relations, can become occasions for announcing and witnessing to the faith. The Holy Father reminds us with these words:

> Peter and the Apostles proclaim courageously, fearlessly, what they have received: the Gospel of Jesus. And we? Are we capable of bringing the word of God into the environment in which we live? Do we know how to speak of Christ, of what he represents for us, in our families, among the people who form part of our daily lives? Faith is born from listening, and is strengthened by proclamation ...
>
> In God's great plan, every detail is important, even yours, even my humble little witness, even the hidden witness of those who live their faith with simplicity in everyday family relationships, work relationships, friendships.[62]

Education

Here are a few lines of suggestions from the Holy Father, inspired by a typically Ignatian spirituality: 'In educating a balance must be maintained, your steps must be well balanced, one step on the cornice of safety but the other into the zone of risk. And when the risk becomes safe, the next step must venture into another area of risk. Education cannot be confined to the safety zone. No. This would mean preventing personalities from developing; yet it is not possible to educate solely in the risk zone either: this is too dangerous. It is a balance of steps: remember it well.'[63]

The pope encourages educators 'to seek new, unconventional forms of education, so as to comply with the needs of places, times and people. This is important; ... always go a step "further" and never be satisfied with conventional things. Seek new forms in accordance with the places, times and people.'[64]

In a message addressed to Muslims on the occasion of the end of Ramadan, the Holy Father speaks about promoting mutual respect, especially through the education of the next generations. He wishes to underline:

> the importance of education in the way we understand each other, built upon the foundation of mutual respect. 'Respect' means an attitude of kindness towards people for whom we have consideration and esteem. 'Mutual' means that this is not a one-way process, but something shared by both sides.
>
> What we are called to respect in each person is first of all his life, his physical integrity, his dignity and the rights deriving from that dignity, his reputation, his property, his ethnic and cultural identity, his ideas and his political choices. We are therefore called to think, speak and write respectfully of the other, not only in his presence, but always and everywhere, avoiding unfair criticism or defamation. Families, schools, religious teaching and all forms of media have a role to play in achieving this goal … Regarding the education of … youth, we have to bring up our young people to think and speak respectfully of other religions and their followers, and to avoid ridiculing or denigrating their convictions and practices.[65]

Pope Francis also views the urgency of education as a delicate question because, 'Young people are particularly sensitive to the empty, meaningless values that often surround them. Unfortunately, moreover, it is they who pay the consequences.'[66] The pontiff's participation at the Twenty-Eighth World Youth Day in Rio de Janeiro, Brazil, 13–28 July 2013, had as its goal that through Mary it 'may help all of us, pastors of God's people, parents and educators, to pass on to our young people the values that can help them build a nation and a world which are more just, united and fraternal'.[67] According to the Holy Father, they need help to 'confront the daily vanity, that poison of emptiness which creeps into our society based on profit and possession and on consumerism which deceives young people'.[68]

He addresses educators in these terms:

> It is true that nowadays, to some extent, everyone, including our young people, feels attracted by the many idols which take the place of God and appear to offer hope: money, success, power, pleasure. Often a growing sense of loneliness and emptiness in the hearts of many people leads them to seek satisfaction in these ephemeral idols. Dear brothers and sisters, let us be lights of hope! Let us maintain a positive outlook on reality. Let us encourage the generosity which is typical of the young and help them to work

actively in building a better world. Young people are a powerful engine for the Church and for society. They do not need material things alone; also and above all, they need to have held up to them those non-material values which are the spiritual heart of a people, the memory of a people.[69]

Pope Francis entrusted care for the participants at the Twenty-Eighth World Youth Day to the bishops and priests who were present in this way:

> Let us help the young. Let us have an attentive ear to listen to their dreams – they need to be heard – to listen to their successes, to pay attention to their difficulties. You have to sit down and listen to the same *libretto*, but accompanied by diverse music, with different characteristics. Having the patience to listen! I ask this of you with all my heart! In the confessional, in spiritual direction, in accompanying. Let us find ways to spend time with them. Planting seeds is demanding and very tiring, very tiring! It is much more rewarding to enjoy the harvest! … Reaping is more enjoyable for us! But Jesus asks us to sow with care and responsibility.
>
> Let us spare no effort in the formation of our young people! … Let us embody this also in our own ministry! To help our young people to discover

the courage and joy of faith, the joy of being loved personally by God, is very difficult. But when young people understand it, when young people experience it through the anointing of the Holy Spirit, this 'being personally loved by God' accompanies them for the rest of their lives. They rediscover the joy that God gave his Son Jesus for our salvation. Let us form them in mission, to go out, to go forth, to be itinerants who communicate the faith. Jesus did this with his own disciples: he did not keep them under his wing like a hen with her chicks. He sent them out! We cannot keep ourselves shut up in parishes, in our communities, in our parish or diocesan institutions, when so many people are waiting for the Gospel! To go out as ones sent. It is not enough simply to open the door in welcome because they come, but we must go out through that door to seek and meet the people! Let us urge our young people to go forth. Of course, they will make mistakes, but let us not be afraid! The Apostles made mistakes before us. Let us urge them to go forth. Let us think resolutely about pastoral needs, beginning on the outskirts, with those who are farthest away, with those who do not usually go to church. They are the VIPs who are invited. Go and search for them at the crossroads.[70]

The Holy Father makes this heartfelt request of the adults who accompanied the young participants in World Youth Day: 'Please, continue to accompany them with generosity and joy, help them to become actively engaged in the Church; never let them feel alone!'[71]

The first international journey of Pope Francis' pontificate was undertaken to participate in the Twenty-Eighth World Youth Day. He speaks about it:

> This first journey is about meeting the young people, but not in isolation from their lives – I would rather meet them within their social context, in society. Because when we isolate the young, we do them an injustice; we take away their 'belonging'. The young do belong, they belong to a family, to a homeland, to a culture, to a faith … They belong in all sorts of ways, and we must not isolate them! But in particular, we must not isolate them from the whole of society! They really are the future of a people: it is true. But not only they: they are the future because they have the strength, they are young, they will go forward …
>
> It is true that the global crisis harms the young. I read last week the percentage of the young without work. Just think that we risk having a generation that has never worked, and yet it is through work that a person acquires dignity by earning bread.

The young, at this moment, are in crisis. We have become somewhat accustomed to this throwaway culture: too often the elderly are discarded! But now we have all these young people with no work, they too are suffering the effects of the throwaway culture. We must rid ourselves of this habit of throwing away. No! The culture of inclusion, the culture of encounter, making an effort to bring everyone into society! This is the meaning I want to give to this visit among the young, the young within society.[72]

The pontiff returns to the subject of youth unemployment in these words: 'The percentage of young people without work that we have is very high; we have a generation that has no experience of the dignity that is earned by working … And so the young people, they need to step up and prove their worth; young people need to come out and fight for values, fight for these values.'[73]

Nor does Pope Francis fail to recall situations of suffering. For example, regarding the spread of drugs and the plague of drug trafficking and the liberalisation of drug use, he believes it is necessary to educate 'young people in the values that build up life in society, accompanying those in difficulty and giving them hope for the future. We all need to look upon one another with the loving eyes of Christ, and to learn to embrace those in need, in order to show our closeness, affection and love.'[74]

Always very attentive to the mundane details of daily life, the Holy Father suggests undertaking concrete attitudes and behaviours. Reflecting on the fact that consumerism has led us to become accustomed to excess and to a 'throwaway culture', he reminds us that 'There was a time when our grandparents were very careful not to throw away any leftover food.'[75]

Dreaming Big

Convinced that 'we must bet on youth for the great ideals',[76] Pope Francis offers them this invitation: 'And you, dear young people, think about the talents God has given you and always have a generous spirit … Especially you, dear young people present here, who are here in such great numbers, I want to encourage you not to bury your talents but to think about how you can help build the Kingdom of God. The Church needs you.'[77] As someone with a profound understanding of the human spirit, the Holy Father recognises that 'the young – all of them – have this wish to be authentic, to be consistent'.[78] Nor does he forget to mention 'how many young people renounce their own interests in order to dedicate themselves to children, the disabled, the elderly …'[79]

Referring to the imminent Twenty-Eighth World Youth Day, the pope reaffirms that everyone who participates in it wants 'to hear the voice of Jesus, to listen to Jesus: "Lord, what should I do with my life?

What is the path for me?"'[80] It might be that 'some of you may not yet know what you will do with your lives. Ask the Lord, and he will show you the way.'[81] He invites them once again to reflect with these words: 'Think of this, ask yourselves this: is Jesus calling me to go forth, to come out of myself to do good? To you, young people, to you boys and girls I ask: you, are you brave enough for this, do you have the courage to hear the voice of Jesus?'[82]

Here is more encouragement to 'ask that same question of the Lord: "Lord Jesus, what should I do with my life? What is the path for me?"'[83] More provocatively, Pope Francis poses this question: 'I ask you who are just setting out on your journey through life: have you thought about the talents that God has given you? Have you thought of how you can put them at the service of others? Do not bury your talents! Set your stakes on great ideals, the ideals that enlarge the heart, the ideals of service that make your talents fruitful. Life is not given to us to be jealously guarded for ourselves, but is given to us so that we may give it in turn. Dear young people, have a deep spirit! Do not be afraid to dream of great things!'[84]

On another occasion, the Holy Father returns to this theme with vigour: 'First of all I would like to say one thing to all you young people: do not let yourselves be robbed of hope! Please, do not let yourselves be robbed of it! And who robs you of hope? The spirit of the world, wealth, the spirit of vanity, arrogance, pride. All these things steal hope from you ... But do not let yourselves be robbed of hope by well-being, by the spirit of well-being which, in the end brings you to become a nothing in life! The young must stake themselves on high ideals: this is my advice.'[85]

Hope was also the subject of the very first message the pope addressed to young people, delivered on the occasion of Easter: 'I say to you: carry this certainty ahead: the Lord is alive and walks beside you through life. This is your mission! Carry this hope onward. May you be anchored to this hope: this anchor which is in heaven; hold the rope firmly, be anchored and carry hope forward. You, witnesses of Jesus, pass on the witness that Jesus is alive and this will give us hope, it will give hope to this world, which has aged somewhat, because of wars, because of evil and because of sin. Press on, young people!'[86]

Still speaking to the young, the pope returns to the theme of vocation:

> Jesus asks us to follow him for life, he asks us to be his disciples, to 'play on his team' ... Now, what do players do when they are asked to join a team? They have to train, and to train a lot! The same is true of our lives as the Lord's disciples. Saint

Paul, describing Christians, tells us: 'Every athlete exercises discipline in every way. They do it to win a perishable crown, but we an imperishable one' (1 Cor 9:25). Jesus offers us something bigger than the World Cup! Something bigger than the World Cup! Jesus offers us the possibility of a fruitful life, a life of happiness; he also offers us a future with him, an endless future, in eternal life. That is what Jesus offers us. But he asks us to pay admission, and the cost of admission is that we train ourselves 'to get in shape', so that we can face every situation in life undaunted, bearing witness to our faith, by talking with him in prayer ... I ask you all ... but reply in the silence of your heart, not aloud: do I pray? Do I speak with Jesus, or am I frightened of silence? Do I allow the Holy Spirit to speak in my heart? Do I ask Jesus: what do you want me to do, what do you want from my life?

This is training. Ask Jesus, speak to Jesus, and if you make a mistake in your life, if you should fall, if you should do something wrong, don't be afraid. Jesus, look at what I have done, what must I now do? Speak continually with Jesus, in the good times and in the bad, when you do right, and when you do wrong. Do not fear him! This is prayer. And through this, you train yourselves in dialogue with Jesus ... By loving one another, learning to listen, to understand, to forgive, to be accepting and to help others, everybody, with no one excluded or ostracised. Dear young people, be true 'athletes of Christ'! ... Dear friends, never forget that you are the field of faith! You are Christ's athletes! You are called to build a more beautiful Church and a better world.[87]

Speaking directly to young people, Pope Francis offers this encouragement: 'To you young people I say: Do not be afraid to go against the current, when they want to rob us of hope, when they propose rotten values, values like food gone bad – and when food has gone bad, it harms us; these values harm us. We must go against the current! And you young people are the first: Go against the tide and have the daring to move precisely against the current. Forward, be brave and go against the tide! And be proud of doing so.'[88]

And again, 'You young people, my dear young friends, you have a particular sensitivity towards injustice, but you are often disappointed by facts that speak of corruption on the part of people who put their own interests before the common good. To you and to all, I repeat: never yield to discouragement, do not lose trust, do not allow your hope to be extinguished. Situations can change, people can change. Be the first to seek to bring good, do not grow accustomed to evil, but defeat it with good.'[89]

The future belongs to the young and thanks to them can make progress towards improvement. This is, after all, what every person aspires to when they consider their life. With these affectionate words, Pope Francis shows that he too shares it:

> Your young hearts want to build a better world. I have been closely following the news reports of the many young people who throughout the world have taken to the streets in order to express their desire for a more just and fraternal society. Young people in the streets. It is the young who want to be the protagonists of change. Please, don't leave it to others to be the protagonists of change. You are the ones who hold the future! You ... Through you the future is fulfilled in the world. I ask you also to be protagonists of this transformation. Continue to overcome apathy, offering a Christian response to the social and political anxieties, which are arising in various parts of the world. I ask you to be builders of the world, to work for a better world. Dear young people, please, don't be observers of life, but get involved. Jesus did not remain an observer, but he immersed himself. Don't be observers, but immerse yourself in the reality of life, as Jesus did.[90]

There are many sad people who have lost hope. 'Think too of the many young people who after trying out so many things, fail to find a meaning for life and opt for suicide as a solution. Do you know how many young people commit suicide in the world today? A large number. Why? They have no hope.'[91] A young person cannot be that way, especially if he or she commits to following Jesus: 'One cannot understand a young person without enthusiasm! Follow the Lord with enthusiasm, let him guide you.'[92]

Like a good father, he affectionately directs this appeal to young men and women, 'Be committed to your daily duties, your studies, your work, to relationships of friendship, to helping others; your future also depends on how you live these precious years of your life. Do not be afraid of commitment, of sacrifice and do not view the future with fear. Keep your hope alive: there is always a light on the horizon.'[93]

Being the protagonist in building a better world means responding to a call: 'Today too, as always, the Lord needs you, young people, for his Church. My friends, the Lord needs you! Today too, he is calling each of you to follow him in his Church and to be missionaries. The Lord is calling you today! Not the masses, but you, and you, and you, each one of you. Listen to what he is saying to you in your heart.'[94]

Our spirit can be beset by contradictions, by a feeling that we are not up to the task. Pope Francis is so aware of this that he offers the following reflections:

> Maybe sometimes we are like the path: we hear the Lord's word but it changes nothing in our lives because we let ourselves be numbed by all the superficial voices competing for our attention. I ask you ... everyone respond in his or her own heart: am I a young person who is numb? Or perhaps we are like the rocky ground: we receive Jesus with enthusiasm, but we falter and, faced with difficulties, we don't have the courage to swim against the tide. Every one of us responds in his or her heart: am I courageous or am I a coward? Or maybe we are like the thorny ground: negativity, negative feelings choke the Lord's word in us (cf. Mt 13:18-22). Do I have the habit of playing both sides in my heart: do I make a good impression for God or for the devil? Do I want to receive the seed from Jesus and at the same time water the thorns and the weeds that grow in my heart? But today I am sure that the seed is able to fall on good soil ... 'No, Father, I am not good soil; I am a disaster, and I am full of stones, of thorns, of everything.' Yes, maybe this is so on the surface, but free a little piece, a small piece of good soil, and let the seed fall there and watch how it grows. I

know that you want to be good soil, true Christians, authentic Christians, not part-time Christians: 'starchy', aloof and Christian in 'appearance only'. I know that you don't want to be duped by a false freedom, always at the beck and call of momentary fashions and fads. I know that you are aiming high, at long-lasting decisions which are meaningful ... if it is true, let us all look into our hearts and each one of us tell Jesus that we want to receive the seed of his Word. Say to him: Jesus, look upon the stones, the thorns, and the weeds that I have, but look also upon this small piece of ground that I offer to you so that the seed may enter my heart ... let us allow the seed of Jesus to enter our hearts ... Allow it to grow, and God will nurture it.[95]

Here are some more of the pontiff's thoughts on the same subject: 'Young people must be strong, nourished by the faith and not filled with other things! "Put on Christ" in your life, place your trust in him and you will never be disappointed! ... Dear friends, faith is revolutionary and today I ask you: are you open to entering into this revolutionary wave of faith? Only by entering into this wave will your young lives make sense and so be fruitful!'[96] 'May the Mother of Jesus teach you, dear young people, the courage to make definitive choices.'[97]

The pope expresses his thanks to young people: 'You bring us the joy of faith and you tell us that we must live the faith with a young heart, always: a young heart, even at the age of seventy or eighty. Dear young people! With Christ, the heart never grows old!'[98] 'The young make everyone feel young.'[99]

The profound trust with which Pope Francis regards young people is based on this certainty:

> Christ offers them space, knowing that there is no force more powerful than the one released from the hearts of young people when they have been conquered by the experience of friendship with him. Christ has confidence in young people and entrusts them with the very future of his mission, 'Go and make disciples.' Go beyond the confines of what is humanly possible and create a world of brothers and sisters! And young people have confidence in Christ: they are not afraid to risk for him the only life they have, because they know they will not be disappointed.[100]

Handing on the Faith

'In the acts of the martyrs, we read the following dialogue between the Roman prefect Rusticus and a Christian named Hierax: "Where are your parents?" the judge asked the martyr. He replied: "Our true father is Christ, and our mother is faith in him" (*Acta Sanctorum*, June, I, 21).[101] For those early Christians, faith, as an encounter with the living God revealed in Christ, was indeed a "mother", for it had brought them to the light and given birth within them to divine life, a new experience and a luminous vision of existence for which they were prepared to bear public witness to the end.'[102]

In the various messages he addresses to pilgrims in different languages at the end of audiences, the pope offers the following good wishes, 'Dear newlyweds, may grace come to you from the Paschal Mystery to make your family a place of faithful, fertile love.'[103] 'May Christ the Good Shepherd … help you, dear newlyweds, to build your family on God's love.'[104] 'May the Risen Lord ... guide you, dear newlyweds, so that your family will grow in holiness, after the model of the Holy Family.'[105]

Mums and dads have a particular role in training their children in faith:

> In the family, faith accompanies every age of life, beginning with childhood: children learn to trust in the love of their parents. This is why it is so important that within their families parents encourage shared expressions of faith which can help children gradually to mature in their own faith. Young people in particular, who are going through a period in their lives which is so complex, rich and important for their faith, ought to feel the constant closeness and support of their families and the Church in their journey of faith. We have all seen, during World Youth Days, the joy that young people show in their faith and their desire for an ever more solid and generous life of faith. Young people want to live life to the fullest. Encountering Christ, letting themselves be caught up in and guided by his love, enlarges the horizons of existence, gives it a firm hope which will not disappoint. Faith is no refuge for the faint-hearted, but something which enhances our lives. It makes us aware of a magnificent calling, the vocation of love. It assures us that this love is trustworthy and worth

embracing, for it is based on God's faithfulness which is stronger than our every weakness.[106]

It is within the family that we are trained for a relationship with the Lord and for conversation with him: 'Ever since we were children, our parents have taught us to start and end the day with a prayer, to teach us to feel that the friendship and the love of God accompanies us.'[107]

Pope Francis illustrates the significance of the sacrament that introduces us to Christian life:

The structure of Baptism, its form as a rebirth in which we receive a new name and a new life, helps us to appreciate the meaning and importance of infant Baptism. Children are not capable of accepting the faith by a free act, nor are they yet able to profess that faith on their own; therefore the faith is professed by their parents and godparents in their name. Since faith is a reality lived within the community of the Church, part of a common 'We', children can be supported by others, their parents and godparents, and welcomed into their faith, which is the faith of the Church; this is symbolised by the candle which the child's father lights from the paschal candle. The structure of Baptism, then, demonstrates the critical importance of cooperation between Church and family in passing on the faith. Parents are called, as St Augustine once said, not only to bring children into the world but also to bring them to God, so that through Baptism they can be reborn as children of God and receive the gift of faith.[108] Thus, along with life, children are given a fundamental orientation and assured of a good future; this orientation will be further strengthened in the Sacrament of Confirmation with the seal of the Holy Spirit.[109]

The Holy Father extends this invitation to everyone: 'It would be nice if, especially in this month of May, we could pray the Holy Rosary together in the family, with friends, in the parish, or some prayer to Jesus and the Virgin Mary! Praying together is a precious moment that further strengthens family life, friendship! Let us learn to pray more in the family and as a family!'[110] He repeats it again, 'I urge you all to learn to pray in the family and as a family! … Reciting the Rosary helps us to stand beside Mary and contemplate the mysteries of Jesus' life.'[111] This invitation is further supported by a small and very personal confession which the pope shares about his prayer to Mary: 'One thing that makes me strong every day is praying the Rosary to Our Lady. I feel such great strength because I go to her and I feel strong.'[112]

St Joseph: Protector of the Family of Nazareth

Pope Francis wished to begin his Petrine ministry on 19 March 2013, the Solemnity of St Joseph, Spouse of the Virgin Mary and Patron of the Universal Church. He makes frequent reference to 'St Joseph who watched over Mary and Jesus, of his care for the family God had entrusted to him, and of the attentive gaze with which he guided it to avoid the perils on the way.'[113] 'Jesus comes into our history, he comes among us by being born of Mary by the power of God, but with the presence of St Joseph, the legal father who cares for him and also teaches him his trade. Jesus is born and lives in a family, in the Holy Family, learning the carpenter's craft from St Joseph in his workshop in Nazareth, sharing with him the commitment, effort, satisfaction and also the difficulties of every day.'[114]

Saint Joseph is the carpenter, 'Jesus' adoptive father' from whom 'Jesus learned to work'.[115] In a long explanation, the Holy Father explores the figure of St Joseph, called to watch over the Holy Family: [53]

> Joseph did as the angel of the Lord commanded him and took Mary as his wife' (Mt 1:24). These words already point to the mission which God entrusts to Joseph: he is to be the *custos*, the protector. The protector of whom? Of Mary and Jesus; but this protection is then extended to the Church, as Blessed John Paul II pointed out: 'Just as St Joseph took loving care of Mary and gladly dedicated himself to Jesus Christ's upbringing, he likewise watches over and protects Christ's Mystical Body, the Church, of which the Virgin Mary is the exemplar and model' (Apostolic Exhortation *Redemptoris Custos*, no. 1).
>
> How does Joseph exercise his role as protector? Discreetly, humbly and silently, but with an unfailing presence and utter fidelity, even when he finds it hard to understand. From the time of his betrothal to Mary until the finding of the twelve-year-old Jesus in the Temple of Jerusalem, he is there at every moment with loving care. As the spouse of Mary, he is at her side in good times and bad, on the journey to Bethlehem for the census and in the anxious and joyful hours when she gave birth; amid the drama of the flight into Egypt and during the frantic search for their child in the Temple; and later

in the day-to-day life of the home of Nazareth, in the workshop where he taught his trade to Jesus.

How does Joseph respond to his calling to be the protector of Mary, Jesus and the Church? By being constantly attentive to God, open to the signs of God's presence and receptive to God's plans, and not simply to his own. This is what God asked of David, as we heard in the first reading. God ... want[s] faithfulness to his word, to his plan ... Joseph is a 'protector' because he is able to hear God's voice and be guided by his will; and for this reason he is all the more sensitive to the persons entrusted to his safekeeping. He can look at things realistically, he is in touch with his surroundings, he can make truly wise decisions.[116]

Saint Joseph assumes his parental role alongside the Madonna. 'In the silence of the daily routine, St Joseph, together with Mary, share a single common centre of attention: Jesus. They accompany and nurture the growth of the Son of God made man for us with commitment and tenderness, reflecting on everything that happened. In the Gospels, St Luke twice emphasises the attitude of Mary, which is also that of St Joseph: she "kept all these things, pondering them in her heart" (2:19, 51).'[117]

Pope Francis adds one further note. 'Caring, protecting, demands goodness, it calls for a certain tenderness. In the Gospels, St Joseph appears as a strong and courageous man, a working man, yet in his heart we see great tenderness, which is not the virtue of the weak but rather a sign of strength of spirit and a capacity for concern, for compassion, for genuine openness to others, for love.'[118]

On the occasion of blessing the new statue of St Michael the Archangel in the Vatican Gardens, the Holy Father entrusts the protection of the Vatican with these words: 'Dear brothers and sisters, let us also consecrate Vatican City State also to St Joseph, the guardian of Jesus, of the Holy Family. His presence helps us to be ever stronger and to have the courage to make space for God in our life so that good may always conquer evil. Let us ask him to keep us, care for us, so that the life of Grace may increase every day in each one of us.'[119]

Mother Mary

The Madonna appears as an exemplary figure right from the moment of the Annunciation: 'Mary … humbles herself: she does not properly understand, but she is free: she grasps only the essential, and says "yes". She is humble: "May God's will be done". She entrusts her soul to God's will. Joseph, her betrothed, also lowers himself and takes this great responsibility upon his shoulders.' Joseph 'also says "yes" to the angel when in his dream the angel tells him of this truth'.[120]

It is well known that Pope Francis has a particular devotion to the Madonna, whom he has repeatedly defined in these terms: 'She is our Mother. Let us entrust ourselves to her, because she cares for us like a *buona mamma* [good mom].'[121] And again: 'For this reason Mary our Mother, Our Lady, shines out for us as a sign of sure hope. She is the Mother of Hope; on our journey, on our way, she is Mother of Hope. She is also the Mother who comforts us, the Mother of consolation and the Mother who accompanies us on the journey. Let us now pray to Our Lady all together, to Our Mother who accompanies us on the way.'[122]

'"Wherever the mother is, there the children are safe" and "if we are afraid, we know that we have our mother with us". Just like children who take refuge in their mother's arms, so too, when "we are a little afraid, we go to her". And, as the most ancient antiphon says, she "guards with her mantle, with her maternal protection".' [123]

'Mary's true motherhood also ensured for the Son of God an authentic human history, true flesh in which he would die on the cross and rise from the dead. Mary would accompany Jesus to the cross (cf. Jn 19:25), whence her motherhood would extend to each of his disciples (cf. Jn 19:26-27). She will also be present in the upper room after Jesus' Resurrection and ascension, joining the apostles in imploring the gift of the Spirit (cf. Acts 1:14).'[124]

As the mother of each of us, the Madonna is at our side in difficult moments such as she herself was not spared. 'Mary saw many difficult moments in her life, from the birth of Jesus, when "there was no place for them in the inn" (Lk 2:7), to Calvary (cf. Jn 19:25).'[125] The Holy Father points out, 'Mary also experienced the martyrdom of the Cross: the martyrdom of her heart, the martyrdom of her soul. She lived her Son's Passion to the depths of her soul. She was fully united to him in his death, and so she was given the gift of Resurrection.

Christ is the first fruits from the dead and Mary is the first of the redeemed, the first of 'those who are in Christ'. She is our Mother, but we can also say that she is our representative, our sister, our eldest sister, she is the first of the redeemed, who has arrived in heaven.'[126] In the struggle against the Evil One, whom:

> the disciples must confront – all of us, all the disciples of Jesus, we must face this struggle – Mary does not leave them alone: the Mother of Christ and of the Church is always with us. She walks with us always, she is with us. And in a way, Mary shares this dual condition. She has of course already entered, once and for all, into heavenly glory. But this does not mean that she is distant or detached from us; rather Mary accompanies us, struggles with us, sustains Christians in their fight against the forces of evil. Prayer with Mary, especially the Rosary … has this 'suffering' dimension, that is of struggle, a sustaining prayer in the battle against the evil one and his accomplices. The Rosary also sustains us in the battle.[127]

Mary's unfailing support is reliable. Pope Francis encourages us:

> Like a good mother she is close to us, so that we may never lose courage before the adversities of life,

before our weakness, before our sins: she gives us strength, she shows us the path of her Son.

Jesus from the Cross says to Mary, indicating John: 'Woman, behold your son!' and to John: 'Here is your mother!' (cf. Jn 19:26-27). In that disciple, we are all represented: the Lord entrusts us to the loving and tender hands of the Mother, that we might feel her support in facing and overcoming the difficulties of our human and Christian journey; to never be afraid of the struggle, to face it with the help of the mother ...

The *Salus Populi Romani* is the mother that gives us health in growth, she gives us health in facing and overcoming problems, she gives us the health to make us free to make definitive choices. The mother teaches us how to be fruitful, to be open to life and to always bear good fruit, joyful fruit, hopeful fruit, and never to lose hope, to give life to others, physical and spiritual life.[128]

Pope Francis reminds us 'The Gospel of St Luke tells us that, in the family of Nazareth, Jesus "grew and became strong, filled with wisdom; and the favour of God was upon him" (Lk 2:40). Our Lady does just this for us, she helps us to grow as human beings and in the faith, to be strong and never to fall into the temptation of being human beings and Christians in a superficial way, but to live responsibly, to strive ever higher.'[129]

God Is a Merciful Father

The Holy Father turns to this image to explain how holding fast to Jesus Christ enables one to overcome human frailty and fear: 'A child is very frail ... but if they're with their father, with their mother, they are safe'.[130]

With the certainty that 'God's love is seen to be like that of a father who carries his child along the way (cf. Dt 1:31)',[131] Pope Francis repeats countless times the invitation to trust in the limitless mercy of God, because 'God's face is the face of a merciful father who is always patient. Have you thought about God's patience, the patience he has with each one of us? That is his mercy. He always has patience, patience with us, he understands us, he waits for us, he does not tire of forgiving us if we are able to return to him with a contrite heart. "Great is God's mercy," says the Psalm ... We need to understand properly this mercy of God, this merciful Father who is so patient ... He is the loving Father who always pardons, who has that heart of mercy for us all.'[132]

Referring to the parable of the prodigal son, the pontiff repeats with particular emphasis:

> God always thinks with mercy: do not forget this. God always thinks mercifully. He is the merciful Father! God thinks like the father waiting for the son and goes to meet him, he spots him coming when he is still far off ...
>
> What does this mean? That he went every day to see if his son was coming home: this is our merciful Father. It indicates that he was waiting for him with longing on the terrace of his house. God thinks like the Samaritan who did not pass by the unfortunate man, pitying him or looking at him from the other side of the road, but helped him without asking for anything in return; without asking whether he was a Jew, a pagan or a Samaritan, whether he was rich or poor: he asked for nothing. He went to help him: God is like this. God thinks like the shepherd who lays down his life in order to defend and save his sheep.[133]

Once again, Pope Francis refers to his personal experience along the journey of faith:

> I am always struck when I reread the parable of the merciful Father; it impresses me because it always gives me great hope. Think of that younger son who

was in the Father's house, who was loved; and yet he wants his part of the inheritance; he goes off, spends everything, hits rock bottom, where he could not be more distant from the Father, yet when he is at his lowest, he misses the warmth of the Father's house and he goes back. And the Father? Had he forgotten the son? No, never. He is there, he sees the son from afar, he was waiting for him every hour of every day, the son was always in his father's heart, even though he had left him, even though he had squandered his whole inheritance, his freedom. The Father, with patience, love, hope and mercy, had never for a second stopped thinking about him, and as soon as he sees him still far off, he runs out to meet him and embraces him with tenderness, the tenderness of God, without a word of reproach: he has returned! …

In my own life, I have so often seen God's merciful countenance, his patience; I have also seen so many people find the courage to enter the wounds of Jesus by saying to him: Lord, I am here, accept my poverty, hide my sin in your wounds, wash it away with your blood. And I have always seen that God did just this – he accepted them, consoled them, cleansed them, loved them.

Dear brothers and sisters, let us be enveloped by the mercy of God; let us trust in his patience, which always gives us more time. Let us find the courage to return to his house, to dwell in his loving wounds, allowing ourselves be loved by him and to encounter his mercy in the sacraments. We will feel his wonderful tenderness, we will feel his embrace, and we too will become more capable of mercy, patience, forgiveness and love.[134]

Once he had returned home, the prodigal son who had squandered his inheritance recognises his error and begs forgiveness: '"Father, I have sinned." This is the key to every prayer: the feeling that we are loved by a father'; and we have 'a Father who is very near to us, who embraces us'. We can unburden ourselves of all our anxieties to him because 'he knows what we need'.[135]
God 'has reconciled the world to himself in Christ, entrusting to us the word of reconciliation. And the grace to carry this word of reconciliation forward forcefully, with the freedom of sons. We have been saved in Jesus Christ.'[136] Through his Death and Resurrection, Jesus has freed us from sin: this is 'the greatest miracle' by which he has made us children of God and has given us the freedom of sons. This is precisely why 'we can say "Father." Otherwise we would not be able to say it … This is the great miracle of Jesus. We who were slaves of sin, he has set free', he has healed us. 'It will do us good to think about this and to consider how good it is to be

sons and daughters. It is so beautiful, this freedom of God's children, because the Son is at home. Jesus has opened the doors of the house to us, and now we are at home. Now we understand this saying of Jesus: "take courage, son, your sins are forgiven." This is the root of our courage: I am free, I am a son, the Father loves me and I love the Father.'[137]

Speaking about the attitude with which we should approach the confessional, the pope reaffirms that God the Father welcomes us in the spirit of Psalm 103: '"As a father has compassion on his children, so the Lord has compassion on those who fear him", those who come to him. The tenderness of the Lord. He always understands us, but he also doesn't give us a chance to speak. He knows everything. "Be calm, go in peace", that peace that only he gives.'[138]

Referring to God's love and how truly He loves us, Pope Francis states, 'God is Father, he loves us as a true father loves.'[139]

'It is the Spirit himself whom we received in Baptism who teaches us, who spurs us to say to God: "Father" or, rather, "Abba!" which means "papa" ["dad"]. Our God is like this: he is a dad to us.'[140] 'Moreover, God treats us as children, he understands us, he forgives us, he embraces us, he loves us even when we err.'[141] In fact, the Gospel bears witness to a compassion that 'is God's love for man, it is mercy, thus the attitude of God in contact with human misery, with our destitution, our suffering, our anguish. The biblical term "compassion" recalls a mother's womb. The mother in fact reacts in a way all her own in confronting the pain of her children. It is in this way, according to Scripture, that God loves us … The Lord always watches over us with mercy; he always watches over us with mercy. Let us not be afraid of approaching him! He has a merciful heart!'[142]

Jesus teaches us how to pray by reminding us that 'the Father who is in heaven knows what you need before you ask him'. Therefore, let our first word be '"Father". This is the key to prayer. Without speaking, without feeling this word, praying is not possible … We must "pray to the Father" who begot us. But this is not all: we must pray "our" Father, that is, not the Father of a generic and too anonymous "all", but the One "who begot you, who gave you life, who gave life to you and me".'[143] It is the Father 'who accompanies you on your way', who 'knows your whole life, all of it'; who knows what 'is good and what is not so good. He knows it all … Unless we begin prayer with this word spoken not by the lips but by the heart, we cannot pray as Christians.'[144]

The Holy Father does not fail to show how God is also mother. 'The Lord is a Father and he says that he will be for us like a mother with her baby, with a mother's tenderness.' 'As when a mother takes her child upon her knee and caresses him or her: so the Lord will do and does with us. This is the cascade of tenderness which gives us much consolation. "As a mother comforts her child, so I will comfort you" (66:13).'[145]

For each of us, God is father and mother as long as we relate to Him with the trusting attitude of children, since, 'It is the heart that counts for God, how open to him we are, whether we are like trusting children.'[146]

Spiritual Fatherhood and Motherhood

Pope Francis encourages and defines fatherhood as 'a gift of God and a great responsibility to give a new life that is an unrepeatable image of God. Don't be afraid of becoming parents. Many of you will certainly become fathers! Remain open to spiritual fatherhood too, a great treasure of our faith. God gives you the riches and the radiation of his fatherhood and fills you with his joy.'[147]

The Holy Father advises those who intend to consecrate themselves in religious life:

> The vow of chastity and the vow of celibacy do not end at the moment the vow is taken, they endure … A journey that matures, that develops towards pastoral fatherhood, towards pastoral motherhood, and when a priest is not a father to his community, when a sister is not a mother to all those with whom she works, he or she becomes sad. This is the problem. For this reason I say to you: the root of

sadness in pastoral life is precisely in the absence of fatherhood or motherhood that comes from living this consecration unsatisfactorily which on the contrary must lead us to fertility. It is impossible to imagine a priest or a sister who are not fertile: this is not Catholic! This is not Catholic![148]

The pontiff underscores that 'all of us, to be mature, must feel the joy of fatherhood'. This also applies in the case of the celibate priesthood because 'fatherhood means giving life to others'. This is why for priests it means 'pastoral fatherhood, spiritual fatherhood', which is always and in any case, 'giving life, becoming fathers'.[149]

In Genesis 15:1-12; 17-18, we read how Abraham 'felt that the Lord loved him deeply, that he had promised him many things, but felt in need of offspring. He felt within him "that cry of nature: I want to have a son".' And so he spoke to the Lord of his 'desire to become a father', he presented this desire. Moreover, as Pope Francis observes, he knew how to defend his family. 'Preparing the sacrifice: he takes animals, cuts them up but the birds of prey swoop down. I find it really moving to see this ninety-year-old man, stick in hand, defending the sacrifice, defending what belongs to him.' It is an image Pope Francis associates with 'a father defending the family', a 'father who knows' what it means to 'defend his children', The Holy Father exhorts that this '"is a grace we priests must implore: the grace of pastoral fatherhood, of spiritual fatherhood". Indeed, although we can all have sins, even many sins, not having spiritual sons and daughters, not becoming pastors, is equivalent to living a life that does not reach "the end but stops half way".'[150]

Turning to the female world, the pope explains:

> The role of women in the Church is not simply that of maternity, being mothers, but much greater: it is precisely to be the icon of the Virgin, of Our Lady; what helps make the Church grow! But think about it, Our Lady is more important than the Apostles! She is more important! The Church is feminine. She is Church, she is bride, she is mother. But women, in the Church, must not only… I don't know how to say this in Italian … the role of women in the Church must not be limited to being mothers, workers, a limited role … No! It is something else! But the popes … Paul VI wrote beautifully of women, but I believe that we have much more to do in making explicit this role and charism of women. We can't imagine a Church without women, but women active in the Church, with the distinctive role that they play. I think of an example which has nothing to do with the Church, but is an historical

example: in Latin America, Paraguay. For me, the women of Paraguay are the most glorious women in Latin America. Are you *paraguayo*? After the war, there were eight women for every man, and these women made a rather difficult decision: the decision to bear children in order to save their country, their culture, their faith and their language. In the Church, this is how we should think of women: taking risky decisions, yet as women. This needs to be better explained. I believe that we have not yet come up with a profound theology of womanhood, in the Church. All we say is: they can do this, they can do that, now they are altar servers, now they do the readings, they are in charge of *Caritas* (Catholic charities). But there is more! We need to develop a profound theology of womanhood. That is what I think.[151]

God's Family

The Church's task is to manifest the merciful countenance of God the Father. 'The Church is a mother: she has to go out to heal those who are hurting, with mercy. If the Lord never tires of forgiving, we have no other choice than this: first of all, to care for those who are hurting. The Church is a mother, and she must travel this path of mercy. And find a form of mercy for all. When the prodigal son returned home, I don't think his father told him: "You, sit down and listen: what did you do with the money?" No! He celebrated!'[152]

According to Pope Francis, the Church is not an organisation but rather 'a mother'.

Speaking to the many mothers present at a celebration of the Eucharist, he asks them directly: 'what do you feel when someone says: "But are you the house coordinator?"' anticipating their obvious response: 'No, I am the mama!' 'And the Church is the mother.' And we, by the power of the Holy Spirit, 'all together, we are one family in the Church who is our mother'.[153]

Pope Francis says:

> And in this way the Church is increasingly a Mother, a Mother of many, many children: she becomes a Mother, ever more fully a Mother, a Mother who gives us faith, a Mother who gives us our identity. But Christian identity is not an identity card. Christian identity means being a member of the Church … for apart from the Church it is not possible to find Jesus. The great Paul VI said: it is an absurd dichotomy to wish to live with Jesus but without the Church, to follow Jesus but without the Church, to love Jesus but without the Church (cf. *Evangelii Nuntiandi*, no. 16). And that Mother Church who gives us Jesus also gives us an identity which is not simply a rubber stamp: it is membership. Identity means membership, belonging. Belonging to the Church: this is beautiful![154]

The Holy Father states that for Israel God is the only Lord. He asks his people to follow him with such faithfulness that 'the Lord likes to compare this road with nuptial love. The Lord calls his Church a bride; our soul, a bride.' That is to say, he speaks about 'a love that greatly resembles nuptial love, the love of faithfulness'.[155]

At the start of a number of catecheses on the mystery of the Church, Pope Francis develops the following reflection on God's plan for humanity:

The Church is rooted in this great plan. She is not an organisation established by an agreement between a few people, but ... she is a work of God, born precisely from this loving design which is gradually brought about in history. The Church is born from God's wish to call all people to communion with him, to friendship with him, indeed, to share in his own divine life as his sons and daughters. The very word 'Church', from the Greek *ekklesia*, means 'convocation': God convokes us, he impels us to come out of our individualism, from our tendency to close ourselves into ourselves, and he calls us to belong to his family.

Furthermore this call originates in creation itself. God created us so that we might live in a profound relationship of friendship with him, and even when sin broke off this relationship with him, with others and with creation, God did not abandon us. The entire history of salvation is the story of God who seeks out human beings, offers them his love and welcomes them. He called Abraham to be the father of a multitude, he chose the People of Israel to make a covenant that would embrace all peoples, and in the fullness of time, he sent forth his Son so that his plan of love and salvation might be fulfilled in a new and eternal Covenant with the whole of humanity.

When we read the Gospels, we see that Jesus gathers round him a small community which receives his word, follows it, shares in his journey, becomes his family, and it is with this community that he prepares and builds his Church.

So what is the Church born from? She is born from the supreme act of love of the Cross, from the pierced side of Jesus from which flowed blood and water, a symbol of the sacrament of the Eucharist and of Baptism. The lifeblood of God's family, of the Church, is God's love which is actualised in loving him and others, all others, without distinction or reservation. The Church is a family in which we love and are loved.

When did the Church manifest herself? ... she became manifest when the gift of the Holy Spirit filled the hearts of the Apostles and spurred them to go out and begin their journey to proclaim the Gospel, spreading God's love.

Still today some say: 'Christ yes, the Church no.' Like those who say 'I believe in God but not in priests.' But it is the Church herself which brings Christ to us and which brings us to God. The Church is the great family of God's children.[156] The Church is the family of Jesus.[157]

In God's plan, humanity is one single family, composed of his children who make up the Church, outside of which it is impossible to be a Christian. Commenting on Jesus' reply when Peter asks him what the salary will be, the reward for having left everything for his sake, the Holy Father reminds us that Jesus assures those who follow him of membership in the 'Christian family'. 'We are all brothers and sisters.'[158]

'The Church, like every family, passes on to her children the whole store of her memories.'[159] From this follows the question posed by Pope Francis:

> Let us ask ourselves today: how much do I love the Church? Do I pray for her? Do I feel part of the family of the Church? What do I do to ensure that she is a community in which each one feels welcome and understood, feels the mercy and love of God who renews life? Faith is a gift and an act which concern us personally, but God calls us to live with our faith together, as a family, as Church. Let us ask the Lord, in a very special way during this *Year of Faith*, that our communities, the whole Church, be increasingly true families that live and bring the warmth of God.[160]

Referring to the theme of the Church as a family, the pope raises the following question: 'Let us ask ourselves today whether we love the Church the way we love our families and whether we are praying for the Church.'[161]

The Whole World Understood as One Big Family

The motherhood of the Church grows and expands over time 'which is not yet finished', driven as it is, not by human forces, but by 'the power of the Holy Spirit'.[162] The dream that God has for humanity 'is to make of us all a single family of his children, in which each person feels that God is close and feels loved by him ... feels the warmth of being God's family'.[163]

Turning his attention to newly ordained priests, the Holy Father reminds them of the goal of their ministry: '*Sharing in* for your part the office of Christ, Head and Shepherd, *in filial communion with your* Bishop and subject to him, strive to bring the faithful together into one family, so that you may lead them to God the Father through Christ in the Holy Spirit.'[164]

Thus, even the whole world is to be understood as one big family: 'We are, after all, a single human family, different in many ways, on the road towards unity, valuing solidarity and dialogue among peoples.'[165] At the same time, Pope Francis poses this troubling question: 'But how will we have unity among Christians if we are not capable of it among ourselves, as Catholics? Or in our families? So many families fight and are divided!'[166]

Endnotes

1. Address on the Occasion the Twenty-Eighth World Youth Day, visit to the community of Varingha, 25 July 2013.
2. Interview with the Archdiocese of Rio's 'Cathedral Radio' Studios, 27 July 2013.
3. Address to the participants in the Thirty-Eighth Conference of the Food and Agriculture Organization of the United Nations (FAO), Clementine Hall, 20 June 2013.
4. Letter to British Prime Minister David Cameron on the Occasion of the G8 Meeting, 17–18 June 2013.
5. Meeting with the bishops of Brazil, Archbishop's House, Rio de Janiero, 28 July 2013.
6. Address on the occasion of the official visit of George Napolitano, President of the Republic of Italy, 8 June 2013.
7. Address to His Grace Justin Welby, Archbishop of Canterbury and Primate of the Anglican Communion, 14 June 2013.
8. General Audience, St Peter's Square, 19 June 2013.
9. Encyclical Letter, *Lumen Fidei*, no. 52.
10. Words on the occasion of the encounter with seminarians and male and female novices, Paul VI Hall, 6 July 2013. Unofficial translation based on Vatican Radio translation.
11. Address on the occasion of the meeting with the volunteers of the Twenty-Eighth World Youth Day, Rio de Janeiro, 28 July 2013.
12. Recitation of the Holy Rosary, Papal Basilica of St Mary Major, 4 May 2013. Italicised phrase is an unofficial translation of the Italian.
13. Press conference during the return flight, Twenty-Eighth World Youth Day, Rio de Janeiro, 28 June 2013.
14. Morning meditation in the Chapel of *Domus Sanctae Marthae*, '*The Wisdom of Christians*', 24 May 2013. Unofficial translation.

15. General Audience, St Peter's Square, 29 May 2013. Unofficial translation.
16. *Angelus*, St Peter's Square, 23 June 2013.
17. *Regina Caeli*, St Peter's Square, 21 April 2013.
18. Recitation of the Holy Rosary, Papal Basilica of St Mary Major, 4 May 2013.
19. Address on the occasion of the visit of Giorgio Napolitano, President of the Republic of Italy, 8 June 2013.
20. Recitation of the Holy Rosary, Papal Basilica of St Mary Major, 4 May 2013.
21. *Regina Caeli*, St Peter's Square, 12 May 2013.
22. Morning meditation in the chapel of the *Domus Sanctae Marthae*, 'God's Time', 27 May 2013. Unofficial translation.
23. Ibid., Libreria Editrice Vaticana (LEV) translation.
24. Encyclical Letter, *Lumen Fidei*, no. 52.
25. Address on the occasion of the welcome ceremony, Garden of Guanabara Palace, Rio de Janeiro, 22 July 2013.
26. Ibid.
27. General Audience, St Peter's Square, 12 June 2013.
28. *Regina Caeli*, St Peter's Square, 5 May 2013.
29. Morning meditation in the chapel of the *Domus Sanctae Marthae*, 'Let's Learn the Language Children Speak', 4 June 2013. Unofficial translation.
30. Ibid., LEV translation.
31. General Audience, St Peter's Square, 3 April 2013.
32. Homily on the occasion of priestly ordinations, St Peter's Basilica, 21 April 2013.
33. Homily for the celebration of Passion and Palm Sunday, St Peter's Square, Twenty-Eighth World Youth Day, 24 March 2013.
34. Address, Vigil of Pentecost with ecclesial movements, St Peter's Square, 18 May 2013.
35. Ibid. Unofficial translation.
36. Address, Vigil of Pentecost with ecclesial movements, St Peter's Square, 18 May 2013.

37. Morning meditation in the chapel of the *Domus Sanctae Marthae*, *'Challenging Jesus'*, 3 May 2013. Unofficial translation.
38. *Regina Caeli*, St Peter's Square, 21 April 2013.
39. *Angelus*, from the balcony of the Archbishop's Residence, Rio de Janeiro, 26 July 2013.
40. Ibid.
41. Press conference during the return flight, Twenty-Eighth World Youth Day, Rio de Janeiro, 28 July 2013.
42. *Angelus*, St Peter's Square, 17 March 2013.
43. Morning meditation in the chapel of the *Domus Sanctae Marthae*, *'The Wisdom of Christians'*, 24 May 2013.
44. Morning meditation in the chapel of the *Domus Sanctae Marthae*, *'Joy in Forbearance'*, 7 May 2013. Unofficial translation.
45. Address on the occasion of the audience with the College of Cardinals, Clementine Hall, 15 March 2013.
46. Address on the occasion of the meeting with seminarians and novices, Paul VI Audience Hall, 6 July 2013.
47. Address on the occasion of the meeting with Brazil's leaders of society, Municipal Theatre, Rio de Janeiro, 27 July 2013.
48. Video message to the faithful of Buenos Aires for the feast of St Cajetan, August 7, 2013.
49. Address on the occasion of the meeting with the young people of Argentina, St Sebastian Cathedral, 25 July 2013.
50. Address on the occasion of the meeting with the bishops of Brazil, Archbishop's House, Rio de Janeiro, 27 July 2013.
51. Meeting with the journalists during the flight to Brazil, 22 July 2013.
52. Address on the occasion of the meeting with young people from Argentina, St Sebastian Cathedral, 25 July 2013.
53. Homily on the occasion of the Holy Mass with the bishops at the Twenty-Eighth World Youth Day, along with priests, religious and seminarians, St Sebastian Cathedral, Rio de Janeiro, 27 July 2013.
54. Interview with the Archdiocese of Rio radio station, 'Cathedral Radio' Studios, Rio De Janeiro, 23 July 2013.

55. Address on the occasion of the visit to the community of Varginha (Manguinhos), Twenty-Eighth World Youth Day, 25 July 2013.
56. Address on the occasion of the visit to the 'Gift of Mary' Homeless Shelter, meeting with the Sisters of Charity, 21 May 2013.
57. *Angelus*, St Peter's Square, 11 August 2013.
58. General Audience, St Peter's Square, 12 June 2013.
59. Morning meditation in the chapel of the *Domus Sanctae Marthae*, *'The "All" and "Nothing" of Christianity'*, 17 June 2013. Unofficial translation.
60. Homily on the occasion of the Holy Mass, imposition of the pallium, and bestowal of the fisherman's ring for the inauguration of the Petrine ministry of the Bishop of Rome, St Peter's Square, 19 March 2013, Solemnity of St Joseph.
61. Address on the occasion of the visit to the Hospital of St Francis of Assisi of the Providence of God Hospital, Rio de Janeiro, 24 July 2013.
62. Homily, Basilica of St Paul Outside the Walls, 14 April 2013.
63. Address to the students of the Jesuit schools of Italy and Albania, Paul VI Audience Hall, 7 June 2013.
64. Ibid.
65. Message to Muslims throughout the world on the occasion of the end of Ramadan ('Id Al-Fitr), 10 July 2013.
66. *Angelus*, St Peter's Square, 4 August 2013.
67. Homily at the Basilica of the Shrine of Our Lady of the Conception of Aparecida, on the occasion of the Twenty-Eighth World Youth Day, Rio de Janeiro, 24 July 2013.
68. *Angelus*, St Peter's Square, 4 August 2013.
69. Homily at the Basilica of the Shrine of Our Lady of the Conception of Aparecida, on the occasion of the Twenty-Eighth World Youth Day, Rio de Janeiro, 24 July 2013.
70. Homily at Mass with bishops, priests, religious, and seminarians, Twenty-Eighth World Youth Day, Cathedral of San Sebastian, Rio de Janeiro, 27 July 2013.
71. Homily, Copacabana Waterfront, Rio de Janeiro, 28 July 2013.

72. Meeting with the journalists during the flight to Brazil, 22 July 2013.
73. Ibid. Unofficial translation.
74. Address on the occasion of the visit to St Francis of Assisi of the Providence of God Hospital, Rio de Janeiro, 24 July 2013.
75. General Audience, St Peter's Square, 5 June 2013.
76. *Regina Caeli*, St Peter's Square, 21 April 2013.
77. General Audience, St Peter's Square, 24 April 2013. Unofficial translation.
78. Address on the occasion of the meeting with seminarians and novices, Paul VI Audience Hall, 6 July 2013.
79. *Angelus*, St Peter's Square, 23 June 2013.
80. *Angelus*, St Peter's Square, 21 July 2013.
81. Address on the occasion of the meeting with the volunteers of the Twenty-Eighth World Youth Day, Pavilion 5 of the Rio Centre, Rio de Janeiro, 28 July 2013.
82. *Angelus*, St Peter's Square, 7 July 2013.
83. *Angelus*, St Peter's Square, 21 July 2013.
84. General Audience, St Peter's Square, 24 April 2013.
85. Address to the students of the Jesuit schools in Italy and Albania, Paul VI Audience Hall, 7 June 2013.
86. General Audience, St Peter's Square, 3 April 2013.
87. Address on the occasion of the prayer vigil with young people, Waterfront of Copacabana, Rio de Janeiro, 27 July 2013.
88. *Angelus*, St Peter's Square, 23 June 2013.
89. Address on the occasion of the visit to the community of Varginha (Manguinhos), Twenty-Eighth World Youth Day, 25 July 2013.
90. Address on the occasion of the prayer vigil with the young people, Waterfront of Copacabana, Rio de Janeiro, 27 July 2013.
91. Address to the participants in the ecclesial convention of the Diocese of Rome, Paul VI Audience Hall, 17 June 2013.
92. General Audience, St Peter's Square, 17 April 2013.
93. General Audience, St Peter's Square, 1 May 2013.
94. Address on the occasion of the prayer vigil with the young people, Waterfront of Copacabana, Rio de Janeiro, 27 July 2013.

95. Ibid.
96. Greeting on the occasion of the welcoming ceremony for the young people, Waterfront of Copacabana, 25 July 2013.
97. General Audience, St Peter's Square, 8 May 2013.
98. Homily on the occasion of the celebration of Palm Sunday of the Passion of the Lord, St Peter's Square, Twenty-Eighth World Youth Day, 24 March 2013.
99. Homily at Mass on the occasion of the Twenty-Eighth World Youth Day, Waterfront of Copacabana, Rio de Janeiro, 28 July 2013.
100. Address on the occasion of the welcome ceremony, Garden of Guanabara Palace, Rio de Janeiro, 22 July 2013.
101. Encyclical Letter, *Lumen Fidei*, no. 5.
102. Ibid.
103. General Audience, St Peter's Square, 27 March 2013. Unofficial translation.
104. General Audience, St Peter's Square, 24 April 2013.
105. General Audience, St Peter's Square, 17 April 2013.
106. Encyclical Letter, *Lumen Fidei*, no. 53.
107. General Audience, St Peter's Square, 1 May 2013.
108. Cf. *De nuptiis et concupiscentia*, I, 4, 5: PL 44, 413: '*Habent quippe intentionem generandi regenerandos, ut qui ex eis saeculi filii nascuntur in Dei filios renascantur.*' (They intend to beget children to be born again, so that those who are born of them as children of this age may be reborn as children of God.)
109. Encyclical Letter, *Lumen Fidei*, no. 43.
110. General Audience, St Peter's Square, 1 May 2013.
111. Ibid. Unofficial translation.
112. Address, Vigil of Pentecost with the ecclesial movements, St Peter's Square, 18 May 2013.
113. Address to participants in the pontifical representatives' days, Clementine Hall, 21 June 2013.
114. General Audience, St Peter's Square, 1 May 2013.
115. Morning meditation in the chapel of the *Domus Sanctae Marthae*, 'No to "Slave Labour"', 1 May 2013.

116. Homily on the occasion of the Holy Mass, imposition of the pallium, and bestowal of the fisherman's ring for the beginning of the Petrine ministry of the Bishop of Rome, St Peter's Square, 19 March 2013.
117. General Audience, St Peter's Square, 1 May 2013.
118. Homily on the occasion of the Holy Mass, imposition of the pallium, and bestowal of the fisherman's ring for the beginning of the Petrine ministry of the Bishop of Rome, St Peter's Square, 19 March 2013.
119. Address on the occasion of the blessing of the new statue of St Michael the Archangel, Vatican Gardens, 5 July 2013.
120. Morning meditation in the chapel of the *Domus Sanctae Marthae, 'The Golden Rule of Humility'*, 8 April 2013.
121. Recitation of the Holy Rosary, Papal Basilica of St Mary Major, 4 May 2013.
122. *Angelus* on the Solemnity of the Most Holy Trinity, St Peter's Square, 26 May 2013.
123. Morning meditation in the chapel of the *Domus Sanctae Marthae, 'Renewal Without Fear'*, 6 July 2013. Unofficial translation.
124. Encyclical Letter, *Lumen Fidei*, no. 59.
125. Recitation of the Holy Rosary, Papal Basilica of St Mary Major, 4 May 2013.
126. Homily on the occasion of the Holy Mass for the Solemnity of the Assumption of the Blessed Virgin Mary, Piazza della Libertà, Castel Gandolfo, 15 August 2013.
127. Ibid.
128. Recitation of the Holy Rosary, Papal Basilica of St Mary Major, 4 May 2013.
129. Ibid.
130. Address, Vigil of Pentecost with the ecclesial movements, St Peter's Square, 18 May 2013.
131. Encyclical Letter, *Lumen Fidei*, no. 12.
132. *Angelus*, St Peter's Square, 17 March 2013.
133. General Audience, St Peter's Square, 27 March 2013.

134. Homily on the occasion of the Papal Mass for the possession of the chair of the Bishop of Rome, Basilica of St John Lateran, 7 April 2013.
135. Morning meditation in the chapel of the *Domus Sanctae Marthae*, 'Pray "Our Father"', 20 June 2013. Unofficial translation.
136. Morning meditation in the chapel of the *Domus Sanctae Marthae*, 'The Freedom of God's Children', 4 July 2013. Unofficial translation.
137. Ibid. Unofficial translation.
138. Morning meditation in the chapel of the *Domus Sanctae Marthae*, 'With Blessed Shame', 29 April 2013. Unofficial translation.
139. General Audience, St Peter's Square, 8 May 2013.
140. General Audience, St Peter's Square, 10 April 2013.
141. Ibid.
142. *Angelus*, St Peter's Square, 9 June 2013.
143. Morning meditation in the chapel of the *Domus Sanctae Marthae*, 'Pray "Our Father"', 20 June 2013.
144. Ibid. Unofficial translation.
145. Homily on the occasion of the Holy Mass with seminarians and novices, St Peter's Basilica, 7 July 2013.
146. General Audience, St Peter's Square, 3 April 2013.
147. General Audience, St Peter's Square, 29 May 2013. Unofficial translation.
148. Address on the occasion of the meeting with seminarians and novices, Paul VI Audience Hall, 6 July 2013.
149. Morning meditation in the chapel of the *Domus Sanctae Marthae*, 'The Joy of (Pastoral) Fatherhood', 26 June 2013.
150. Ibid.
151. Press conference during the return flight, Twenty-Eighth World Youth Day, Rio de Janeiro, 28 July 2013.
152. Ibid.
153. Morning meditation in the chapel of the *Domus Sanctae Marthae*, 'A Story of Love', 24 April 2013.
154. Homily on the occasion of the Eucharistic concelebration with the eminent cardinals resident in Rome on the Feast of St George, 23 April 2013.

155. Morning meditation in the chapel of the *Domus Sanctae Marthae*, '*Unmasking the Hidden Idols*', 6 June 2013. Unofficial translation.
156. General Audience, St Peter's Square, 29 May 2013.
157. Morning meditation in the chapel of the *Domus Sanctae Marthae*, '*The Scandal of the Incarnation*', 1 June 2013.
158. Morning meditation in the chapel of the *Domus Sanctae Marthae*, '*The Disciples' Payment*', 28 May 2013. Unofficial translation.
159. Encyclical Letter, *Lumen Fidei*, no. 40.
160. General Audience, St Peter's Square, 29 May 2013.
161. Ibid. Unofficial translation.
162. Morning meditation in the chapel of the *Domus Sanctae Marthae*, '*A Story of Love*', 24 April 2013. Unofficial translation.
163. General Audience, St Peter's Square, 29 May 2013.
164. Homily on the occasion of priestly ordinations, Vatican Basilica, 21 April 2013. Italicised phrases are an unofficial translation of the Italian.
165. Address to the participants of the plenary session of the Pontifical Council for the Pastoral Care of Migrants and Travellers, Clementine Hall, 24 May 2013. Unofficial translation.
166. General Audience, St Peter's Square, 19 June 2013.